ESSENCE
OF LIFE

Poetry & Life in Motion II

Jennifer Fahie

STRATTON
—PRESS—
Publishing Life

ESSENCE OF LIFE
Copyright © 2021 **Jennifer Fahie**

Stratton Press Publishing
831 N Tatnall Street Suite M #188,
Wilmington, DE 19801
www.stratton-press.com
1-888-323-7009

ISBN (Paperback): 978-1-64895-590-7
ISBN (Ebook): 978-1-64895-591-4

Printed in the United States of America

Contents

Mr. Right
(Don't Wait for Him)

On vacation enjoying the ride,
Wishing you were here by my side.

Looking, hoping to see your face in the crowd,
It would be so wonderful I would scream out loud.

If we didn't ride on ExtraTERRORestrial,
Haunted Mansion, or Space Mountain,
We would hold hands and drink from the fountain.

Sitting at the villa, having room service for two,
Eating dessert or getting a drink on you.

Being up early to take my daily run,
Coming back for you to take a swim, shower, or just have fun.

Rowing out on the lake,
That would be just great.

If we went to Busch Gardens, and I tried to get you on Montu,
What in the world would you do?

Looking at the couples on the ride,
Makes me feel funny inside.

Tidal wave might not be your place,
So I will take you on the track for a race.

Feeding the birds, feeding the fish,
Maybe we can catch one and make a dish.

Reminiscing and listening to old music,
Knowing if I ask for a dance, you won't refuse it.

You are with me at work and play,
Thoughts of you make my day.

I pray for you night after night,
Hoping you are the man they call Mr. Right.

True Friend

Our time together was really short,
But that was the moment you stole my heart.

You were as quiet as anyone could be,
But that was what I wanted to see.

You combed my hair and made me feel special,
The job you did was very exceptional.

When I ached and hurt so much,
You massaged me with the magic touch.

We listened to music of old,
You opened this heart of gold.

We read labels at the store,
Being noble, you opened the door.

We drove far to get to the mall,
But when we got there, we had a ball.

The dance we had was short and sweet,
Even though you had two left feet.

We cuddled and watched videos at night.
The company was just out of sight.

To the airport, we drove the next day,
Could you tell I wanted to stay?

Oceans and worlds apart,
But we would always have each other's heart.

We had grown with time,
Always being there for each other on a drop of a dime.

We kept in touch every year,
You always called to show you care.

A precious friend you would always be,
With you I would always have a guarantee.

Disconnected

After meeting you I became possessed,
My feelings put me to the test.

I wanted to speak to you every day,
I wanted to be with you in every way.

When I could not take it anymore,
I started to break down for sure.

I tore your address up and threw it out the door,
I smashed my cell phone on the floor.

I had to erase you from my life,
Because it was always full of strife.

I had to sit and reassess,
I had to know that I was the best.

I put my faith in God,
I prayed and I prayed hard.

Understanding and wisdom was what I got,
It finally put me to this spot.

Now I do not worry if you ever call,
I don't have a problem staring at my wall.

God is always on my side.
And I know where he will abide.

Grow Up, My Sister

Why wait for your child to say, "I love you"?
Why wait for him to say, "I care"?
You need to take the time to find out the burdens that he bears.

One blood, one family,
Respect him, and he will respect you,
Protect him, and he will do the same thing too.

Show him you appreciate him,
And stand by his side,
You should have nothing to hide.

Help him to be all he can be,
And one day, you will see,
The gratitude he shows will break your heart,
It is a feeling that can't be bought.

The closeness that you feel,
Will be the real deal,
Oh! How good it is to love,
It's a gift from our Savior above.

Gone to a Better Place

I always thought we would be together again,
Not knowing it would come to an end.
The day the father would call you home,
And you would no longer be free to roam.

I remember you every day,
When we used to sit on the bay.
You always said I was three times a lady,
I like the way you called me baby.

I remember how we used to dance the night away,
We never stopped until the break of day,
Baby, you were my first,
It was never lust.

After three years apart,
We met again and gave our hearts.
We put our achievements on hold,
Eleven years later, the story should have been told.
Our love will never grow cold.

I dreamed of it being great,
But then the father opened the gate,
He said, "He could no longer wait."

You're in a better place,
Where I can no longer see your face.
I think about you all the time,
I just can't get you off my mind.

Togetherness

A pleasure walk in the park,
A kiss so passionate in the dark.
That's how I'd like it to be,
Spiritual and free.

Meeting your mother and your father,
Your sister, brother, and any other.
Resting on the seventh day,
Rolling around in the hay.

A barbecue in the yard,
And maybe a game of card.
Respecting you in every way,
And loving you day after day.

Sticking together when times get rough,
Bonding more tightly and being tough.
With me you will never be alone,
Because you will always have a home.

The Ultimate Vacation

Have you ever gone away on the ultimate vacation?
Showing true love and dedication.

Doing things you always wanted to do,
Not stopping until the day was through.

Enjoying yourself in the casino all night
Dancing away until the morning light.

Climbing the falls in Jamaica?
Floating out to sea where the waters said, "Let me take her."

Having someone right by your side,
Your face lit up, and the smiles you could not hide.

Coming back to get in the swing of things,
Just to find out that they clipped your wings.

The job you had no longer exist,
Boy! You know I was pissed.

Being dropped in this dilemma,
It was something I would always remember.

Hearing the rumors and the signs on the doors,
To all employees, we are now closed.

Spain

Swinging by my legs from a tree,
Watching the cat licking its knee.
Walking through the Indian graveyard,
Seeing the artifacts, that was hard.

Imagine the culture that had passed,
It was like no other, what a blast!
Going to Oktoberfest,
Boy! That place was blessed.

It made me try things, it made me laugh,
The way they ran, it was sheer craft.
Watching the bull fight up until night,
Hoping those runners ate very light.

The coconut trees were tall and strong,
Lining the waterfront, the street was long.
The ocean looked so nice,
Yet the water was as cold as ice.

The beaches sandy and white,
Everything looked so bright.
Each hotel style was unique,
With pools on the roof to soak your feet.

It was fun to visit another man's land,
To help you see how the world went hand in hand.

Easter Festival of Praise

It was Easter night,
The lights had never seemed so bright.
Off to the Methodist Church, I went,
Even though that was not my intent.

When the United Voices started to sing,
It was such a wonderful thing.
The white guy in the group sang as if he was black,
Man! He almost gave me a heart attack.

The room seemed to be filled with angels on high,
The building felt like a palace floating in the sky.

It made me think about the coming of the Lord,
My Jehovah, my God.

No Matter the Age

I saw him, and I knew he belonged to someone else,
I got to know him, and I knew he would bring me happiness.

I made time for him,
And he responded with kindness.

He looked into my soul, into my heart,
He made me feel we were of the same body part.

Age doesn't matter,
Nor time a factor.
We do not care what the weather,
When we are together.

Thank God for the moments shared,
No matter how crazy or weird.

Your Trip

You've gone on a trip,
Have fun and let it rip.
It's hard, and I can't help but miss,
Your sweet love, affection, and tender kiss.

I miss your voice, your laughter too,
But what am I supposed to do?
I stare at your picture from day to day,
And there are some things I'd like to say.

You're with your son, and I know that,
I'm sitting here eating and getting fat.
I should have let my feelings show,
There are things I should have let you know.

I care for you, and I wish you were here,
I love you, darling; I love you, dear.
Hurry home and see me soon,
So I can stop howling at the moon.

I feel so lonely, tension great,
I just can't wait for our first date.

Missing You

I hear your laughter in the hall,
I look around to see your picture on the wall.

I smell your cologne in the wind,
Make me wonder if I am having a fling.

I feel your presence over me,
I look around, but you I cannot see.

I feel your hand touch my face,
At times, I even feel a warm embrace.

I hear you whispering my name,
I jump around, am I insane?

Why do I think so much about you?
Do you think I am losing a screw?

I plan our wedding in my head,
I am concerned about what the guests will be fed.

We will have the wedding on the lawn,
Then by noontime, we will be gone.

It will be wonderful to be your wife,
We will have had a beautiful life.

Life has taught me not to wait,
We should have set that wedding date.

Live for today and not tomorrow,
'Cause it might just bring you sorrow.
Now that all is said and done,
I will go outside and get some sun.

Surprised

It was your birthday, and I remember,
Just like Christmas in December.
I tried to find a present that was right,
I tried to find something that was out of sight.

I wanted something you would appreciate,
Something that was not out-of-date,
Something that you would remember,
From January down to December.

I wanted something to make you smile,
When you sit down and study, it would make you laugh for a while.
Something in which the memory would last,
Something you think about in the future as well as in the past.

From your reaction, I guess the job was done,
I was surprised you even think of it on the run.
I hope next year you will be even more surprised,
And I'll find something that will open your eyes.

Age

I used to like to party,
Have some drinks and eat heartily.

I thought a handsome guy was all you need,
To make people stand up and take heed.

Having a partner who was good in bed,
Something that went to the head.

Going to every pan that knock,
We thought that really rocked.

Now being halfway through my age,
I look at life from a different stage.

Right now, I hate to be stalked,
All I want is a walk in the park.

I take pride in making someone smile,
Even if it's for a little while.

Hearing laughter in the hall,
That to me is having a ball.

To have a friend when you grow old,
Is the type of story that should be told.

When your legs don't work like they did before,
And you ache so much you rather not go to the store.

Remember the young ones you left behind,
And thoughts of not being kind.

When your eyes are fading, and you can't see,
They will tell you let them be.

Remember the children are our future; treat them well,
So they don't tell you go to hell.

Pisces

I never pay attention to any signs,
But I know about Pisces because it is mine.

We love hard, and we love strong,
And we want it to last long.

We are easygoing and often get hit,
With lies, betrayal, and bullshit.

We must have a sign on our back,
Use me, use me, I think that is a fact.

No matter how many times you push me down,
I will always get up to wear the crown.

Live this life the best you can,
Without despising your fellow man.

No matter what is sent your way,
Always remember to pray, pray, pray.

Training Camp

We came to train with other troops,
It was like jumping through hoops.

They never wanted socialization,
We wondered if we were another nation.

Roving duties with a Texan,
I mistook him for a Mexican.

The heat by day was taking a toll,
The snakes by night would unfold.

Digging foxholes was a reality,
With that heat, it should be human brutality.

The trees were tall and nicely shaped,
But with shingles, it was draped.

Communication was not the best,
It was like two nations: one east, one west.

Finally, the Texans came around,
But by then, we were homeward bound.

Little Things

I could be sitting on my bed,
You could be combing and scratching my head.

Watching a movie was always great,
Having dinner out on the lake.

Putting your arm around my side,
That was when my emotions just couldn't hide.

Kissing me gently on my cheek,
That was when my knees began to feel weak.

Looking up at the beauty of the sky,
Glancing at you starring me straight in my eye.

Life with you could never be boring,
You made me feel like an eagle soaring.

Giving new meaning to everything,
You brought me pleasure in winter as well as spring.

Please don't ever change your game,
Encourage other to be the same.

A treasure is what you are,
Exceptionally the best by far.

Seasons

We don't have winter,
We don't have snow,
We don't have temperatures low.

Summer is ours to have and hold,
The beaches to swim and be bold.
Our leaves don't fall,
And the hark doesn't call.

Our flowers are colorful.
Our grass is green,
Make you want to look at the whole scene.

The sand is white,
On the ocean floor.
Our coral reefs or something to adore.

You can smell the local cuisine,
Your food can be cooked fresh on the scene.

The island is absolutely great,
You might be surprised to pick up a date.
Come see us today the latter part of April to May,
The Virgin Islands the place to play.

Children Are the Future

Nourish children with the Word of God,
Especially now that times are hard.

Help them in the way they should grow,
Do not let our young ladies move from
hand to hand and door to door.

Our boys, the reckless breed,
Help them to be strong and take heed.

Don't let them go astray,
Train them in the right way.

Don't take racism of the past,
You are setting them up for failure, and they won't last.

Try to keep them on the right track,
Always watching each other's back.

Implore our children to prepare for their youths,
Help them to live in harmony, love, and truth.

Prepare them for the journey ahead,
They take over when we are dead.

Each one needs to teach one, it's no mystery,
That is how we preserve our history.

Someday when they are old,
They will see the story unfold.

Remember the children are the future,
We are the past,
Let us help to make our generation last.

Selfishness

You always think about yourself,
Everyone else can sit on a shelf.

You never see yourself as being wrong,
'Cause you figure you are handsome and strong.

You always do the things you want,
You always walk around and flaunt.

So why do you cry when you are treated wrong,
When you always treat others with harm.

You look down on the way people dress,
Thinking you are better than the rest.

Life for you is just a game,
For me, your life is such a shame.

People will always hang around you in a crowd,
They don't always praise you because you're loud.

Do you think anyone will commit to you?
Honey, there are very few.

True love is hard to find,
If you want it, you need to be kind.

What you want is staring you right in the face,
But even this, you cannot embrace.

There has never been no I in us,
I believe in God; you need to trust.

People you should never take for granted,
'Cause we all came from that very seed that was planted.

Near-Death Experience

I was eighteen when I went to my first J'ouvert jam,
So many people, the place was crammed.
Heard a vibration of something hitting an aluminum pole,
Just then the music started to unfold.

Tramping and dancing up the main street,
Being mindful of others dancing offbeat.
Started to sweat, so I took my hand and wiped my brow,
Could not see my hand 'cause the crowd did not allow.

I felt more and more sweat,
I used the other hand 'cause the first one was wet.
Screams came from around me in the crowd,
Man, it was scary and loud.

Someone rushed to me holding a sweater,
By this time, my face grew wetter and wetter.
A Volkswagen drove through the crowd beside me,
But their intentions I could not see.

I asked, "What is going on here?"
The driver answered, "You have been hit, my dear."
I held my hands up to look at them,
I asked myself, "Who!" "What!" and "When!"

Blood streaming down my head,
I thought I was already dead.
They put me in the car, and off to the hospital I went,
Not knowing if I had a cent.

They injected my head with needles and stitched it up,
A crater was left where you could insert a handle of a cup.
I left the hospital that day,
Trying to get home, but I did not know the way.

I saw someone I thought I knew,
So I followed him to see if I could get a clue.
He walked for a while, but I did not stop,
It seemed to me we walked more than a block.

He soon came to a house and went inside,
I sat down outside and only sighed.
I heard a voice calling someone by name,
But I could not tell from whence it came.

I could not imagine who it could be,
But all the tracks led back to me.
A female held my hand and led me inside,
Feeling of embarrassment, I could not hide.

As I entered, I was taken to a bed,
A day later, I got up holding my head.
After listening to every voice,
In my heart, I started to rejoice.

I had followed a stranger, and that was a hunch,
It led me to my sister one of the bunch.
With all that had happened in those two days,
I was so happy to give God the praise.

God's time is never late,
We just need to trust him and have faith.

You Are Their Friend, but They Are Not Yours

There will always be people no matter how hard you try,
They do not appreciate you until you die.
They run to you for comfort and to be held tight,
When problems arise, you hear from them day and night.

You will send a greeting to their phone,
They will act as if the number is unknown.
You will call and you will inquire,
While they look at the number and conspire.

When they are hungry, they will ask you to cook so they can eat,
Never complimenting you after standing at the heat.
Favors are what they think you are there to carry out,
They know you will do it without any doubt.

You are like a well-trained dog,
While they enjoy acting like a hog.
Their manners are very few,
Until there is something else for you to do.

Not because he is well-dressed, handsome, and tall,
That is not love at all.
Love is patient, love is kind.
Tell that man to scatter his behind.

You have a higher calling,
Do not stay there being abused and bawling.
That is not the way life should be,
Be still dear soul and you will see.

Quote Isaiah 60:22,
"When the time is right,
I the Lord will make it happen."

Trials

When trying to do something good in life,
Be prepared to go through headache, pain, and strife.

No matter how simple it might be,
It's like going to college to get a degree.

Trying to write a simple thing,
It will make you crazy, lazy and feel like doing nothing.

If you desire to build a house,
The contractor will play with you like a cat with a mouse.

If you want to buy a piece of land,
The realtor will give you anything to get it off his hand.

If you want to write a book,
When going to the publishers, you must look, look, look.

Make sure they say what you intended,
And people can comprehend it.

When you are booking a trip,
Don't let them talk you into Africa instead of Egypt.

It's not easy being a movie star,
Make sure you are expressed by far.

Life is not as simple as you think,
But hold on, don't take that extra drink.

Please don't go and smoke that crack,
Because it will lay you on your back.

When things get real bad.
Remember, Jesus is all you had.

We pray day and night, not seeing our situation mend,
So we decided this is where the wheel bend and the story end.

Then there's always that last straw that breaks the camel's back,
That's when we know we are under attack.

This happens to the best of us,
Do not give up, do not get disgust.

There will be trials, and we will fall,
The book of James tells it all (James 1:2–4).

And when your back is against the wall,
He will be waiting to hear your call.